CONSTIMOCRAZY:
Malafricanising Democracy

By Nsah Mala

ISBN-13: 978-0-9988476-6-5
ISBN-10: 0998847666
for more books, visit Pski's Porch:
www.pskisporch.com

Printed in U.S.A.

Vices and hardships are the fertile soils on which saints should grow as they strive to reverse the trends. If you lose your sainthood to these things, be warned that hereafter there are no witnesses to justify personal weaknesses.

— Nsah Mala, 2016

Contents

PART ONE
Ragtag: Back and Forth

PART TWO
Constimocrazy: In and Out

PART ONE

Ragtag: Back and Forth

The Torch Ahead

I sometimes live in darkness,
but never do I fear anything.
Through all odds, I see greatness.
And I always try a novel thing.
Hurdles sprout all the times,
but I exploit them in my favour.
So, regardless of the climes,
I urge you to strive for genuine honour.
Behold the torch ahead,
though at times it seems invisible.
Keep leaping and jumping ahead
like a rabbit and never be invincible.
Harness all your talents into hooks
and become balm to human wounds.
Do I not scribble countless books
in the hope to one day earn my pounds?

(Mbankolo, 2016)

Atlantic Shores

On Senegalese Atlantic shores,
we trod on ageless sands,
mounted immortal stones,
swam in wandering waters –
salty, secretive waters
who alone know how many
African slaves crossed the oceans,
how many were pushed into water,
how many died and were food to fish,
how many were raped and thrashed,
how many were killed and thrown off.
As we held hands
and scurried before camera lenses
like newlyweds,
the generous tropical Sun
breathed forth its warmth on us
to protect us against
gentle, cold slaps from Wind,
and my heart wondered if
the Sun and the Moon
can one day release horrendous secrets
blurring black existence
since the encounter with
the Rest.
Thank God, YALI
reminded us of ancestral pardon
in our struggle to uplift
Africa from the dungeons
of stagnation and retrogression!

(Perpignan, 30 December 2016)

Approaching Gorée Island

On a boat piloted by a woman,
we sailed out for Gorée Island
where slaves were not human
when carted away from our land,
loaded full in foreign vessels
like tilapia in fishing boats.
As our boat danced across water,
we saw birds land and take off
in joyful swarms in search of
innocent young fish murdered
by reckless, greedy fishermen.
Soon we halted on Gorée shores
booming in free men and women
where freedom was luxury years ago.

(Perpignan, 1 January 2017)

Spellbound African Dance

One night,
at Framissima Hotel,
in Dakar,
I watched an electrifying dance.
Dancers toyed with fire,
swallowing and spitting it,
passing it through dancing apparel.
They vibrated and turned their buttocks,
conjugating footsteps and body movements
with ancestral drums in hands chiselled
by years of eternal drumming
and responding to sounds of
African cultures droning in their blood veins.
They were
cultural bar magnets to
all onlookers, kept under an irresistible spell
to clap, to nod, to move, to dance, to watch
at no command!
I was one of the imprisoned onlookers,
enticed, entrapped and held by the dance,
not as a musical slave,
but as a cultural addict.

(Perpignan, 30 December 2016)

Treading on Nachtigal's Trails

My trip took me through forests,
filled with slim trees, numbered shrubs;
but not like our forests with bulky trees—
both trees and shrubs unnumbered
yet highly coveted, lusted after!

We also drove through houses
roofed with German immortal zinc.
Don't I remember PM's Lodge Buea,
ENS Bambili with roofs older than WWI?
This WWI that divorced us, began freeing us!

We've been to sacred intellectual groves:
BIGSAS and Bayreuth University—
and I have tasted the nkang of their wisdom,
but not in our horn-cups, calabash-cups, and gourds.
I celebrate this mix, these discoveries, and yet am me!

We've walked Bayreuth streets and roads
under smiling sun rays, and cleansing drizzles
and we've also pedalled on Bismarck's soils
under cold moon rays, and brotherly bulbs.
And we've seen musical acrobatics beneath

nocturnal neons, shaking our own bodies
like proud African lizards, yet praying for a humble heart.
You can't appreciate some meals
until you eat them far from home,
after many months of missing them: eru!

(Bayreuth, 30 October 2016)

Hills and Plains

I've seen humans look alike.
Sometimes, genetics can explain,
they say. Or they claim?
But when hills and plains look alike,
how do we explain? Earth genetics?
When in Scotland
I behold Aberdeen hills with flat heads
filled with same green hair
like Ijim Plateau in Cameroon,
with tree leaves dancing same
music from winds as elsewhere,
to whom goes the credit?
When in France
we drive along sleeping plains,
snoring like Ndop plains in Cameroon
as wind and rice kiss themselves,
to whom goes the credit,
if not to Hands from above?
I've seen hills and plains
in Mbesa and in Dundee
that look like Shakespeare's
famous apple cleft in two
and I can't fail to ask – like Blake –
Beautiful hills and plains,
Dost thou know who made thee?
Beautiful hills and plains,
He calls Himself a Lamb
and a Lamp indeed He is.

(St Andrews, 14 September 2017)

I Jogged into Mother Nature
(After my first jogging sport in St Andrews)

I'm afraid to feel like a rapist;
having raped Nature this morning,
but I was not first jogger on this path.
Once off from the tarred winding track,
I landed on an untamed pathway
that weaves along scanty bushes –
sometimes looking healthy,
sometimes looking like starving kids –
enlivened by rabbits skipping from place
to place along beautiful trails wrapped
across and between shrubs and grasses.
Oh! What a charming muddy-dusty footpath
that transported me, through the airports
in my mind, to Ijim on Mbesa-Belo road!
You think I could overcome the temptation
to chase the rabbits for fun and for food?
(But I didn't catch even one of their tails!)
You think I could overcome the temptation
to watch my past streaming on flat-screens
anchored within me? Sweating now in sports,
sweated then under heavy bags of crops for sale!
Each slippery spot reminded me how many times
I glided and fell under corn or beans or oranges:
the crops that have propelled me into now.
The three golfing men who greeted me
brought memories of Yaoundé Golf Club,
except that those in Yaoundé never greeted us!
Then I descended downhill and crossed a fence
like those we crossed at Ibal-Adamu or Ijim
on our way to Fundong; a signpost announced

that cattle is grazed there in winter, but I wasn't
afraid as we used to fear cattle back home.
To the ocean shores I headed in boundless joy,
halted for selfies on ageless rocks and pebbles;
as I bent to taste the salty waters beneath,
I saw smiling waves rushing to splash and clean
the rocks, bringing along snail-shells and cowries.
Oh! How guilty I felt in Man's place, like a rapist,
to notice waves enraged by our infinite stomachs
seize nets from greedy fishermen, bundle and hurl
them onto seashores for hygiene and sustainability.
When there is no human in sight to learn these,
the baby stream nearby continues to chuckle
down into the ocean as witness that if Man
handles Nature like an egg, all hopes will flourish
like dry-season tomatoes farmed on a swamp!

(St Andrews, 18 March 2017)

Think When Consuming!
(For Prisca Ansama & Blasius D. Akongha)

Mother Earth is no eternal milk-loaded cow
under which hungry calves copiously suck,
pulling & pushing breasts, milk drops wandering
down their innocent cheeks; yet no thoughts
for tomorrow as they forget lurking droughts
that come with every dry season.
We all have awoken to the last cries
of a strangling Earth, wailing in the hands
of greed and uncalculated extractivism.
We can't eat again like my mom in her childhood,
who always wanted to dispose of her leftover food,
& would later devour the same food without remorse
from her brother who had deceived her into
believing he was helping her to throw it way.
We all have awoken to the last snuffles
of a collapsing Earth, weakened by humankind,
who place their luxurious cushions of capitalism
on thin layers covering hungry-angry eco-abysses.
Mother Earth is preparing an ominous will for
our inheritance, except we THINK when consuming.

(St Andrews, 14 March 2017)

Married Off Against Her Will

She didn't know when her bride price was paid;
she was auctioned to a wealthy man before birth.
At puberty, "Meet you husband!" her parents said.
She was given away like a doll prior to its death.
She didn't see the contents of her bride price;
she was sold off to a rich man in her own absence.
When mature, she learned it included wine, goats, rice…
Corpses' hospital bills are not paid in their presence!
She didn't know the exact amount of the money;
she was offered out of her will to a family friend.
At maturity, she was narrated the pomp of the ceremony.
She was treated like a commodity to maintain a friend.
She didn't study to know her imposed husband;
she was given out to repay a debt her father owed.
Her parents presumed they had mastered her husband.
She was taken for a wife whose feelings were borrowed.
She didn't want her husband but was forced to love him.
Though their marriage survived, it was void of happiness.
Her parents and countless others push their girls to the rim
and most of their conjugal lives are draped in bitterness.

(Mbankolo, 14 February 2016, Val's Day)

For Those Who Marry Girls

Don't undress before her.
Take a look at her tender hands,
soft cheeks, innocent face, and soft body.
Isn't your granddaughter older than her?
Pull up your trousers and zip it.
Look at her again: her trembling lips,
teary eyes, spots reddened by your punches.
Why do you want to tear her, grandfather?
This is not marriage; it is child abuse.
The drought of shame in your conscience
must be worse than water drought in the Sahara.
This is not marriage; it is child murder.
Have you once imagined the pangs of trauma
inflicted on the girls you claim to marry?

(St Andrews, 24 March 2017)

The Refugees

Wealthy at first were all refugees.
Ancestral blessings have been on all refugees.
Out of their abodes, something pulled them:
natural – earthquake, flood, eruption, tsunami…
man-made – strike, coup, war, terrorism…
War and terror are the worst of them all.
When on the way out, no eye looks back again:
only mouths may mutter, O God! O God! O God!
Muddy and dusty feet, little and ageless infants,
hearts panicking, watery eyes, dry lips…
Here they are, in a new and foreign land.
Though received with warmth, and resentment at times,
they are shy and their hearts are filled with shame
for it isn't their land, anyway…
Bath, walk, speak, eat…they do without choice.
Bodies and persons worldwide come to their aid,
taking them for babies, but they are world-less there
since choice is no longer theirs.
One day if their problem is solved,
they'll hope to see darling ones who remained afield
and to meet their abodes or rubbles thereof.
In joy and fear, they all dare homeward.
Undigested troubles will deliver unfortunate ones
whose aid can only be SORRY, even from above.
They'll march ahead either to the world of phantoms
or to their nouveau village natal.

(Njinagwa, 21 February 2007)

Humans For or Against Humans?

Behold human skulls shattered
by brotherly bullets spewing
blood-mixed marrow on roads
like broken calabashes vomiting
water or nkang when they fall.
Grounded infants and adults
under rubble; iron birds farting
out mortal smokes above tumbling,
tumbling buildings, tumbling humanity.
Tyrants and tycoons smile before screens.
Future combatants of climate change
crushed beyond recognition or identification.
Enemies of humanity press machine buttons,
churning out bombs and guns for sale,
sponsoring and mocking the peace tale.
Blinded by ignorance, angry protesters
set car tyres in wild flames that eject gases
to rescue Ozone, to save mankind, to destroy.
Kids raising hands to wipe blood on their faces
go viral online, but wars continue offline.
Tsunamis, earthquakes, cyclones and floods
hold emergency meetings to erase humanity.
Ebola, HIV, Malaria, Typhoid…fulfil Malthus.
Yet many seem blind to warring absurdity.
Don't we know that violence is out of fashion?

(Perpignan, 29 December 2016)

Who Hates Mankind?

Ask me who hates mankind?
I will point to those who
take glory in inventing weapons
and measure progress in missiles.
Ask me who hates mankind?
I will point to those who
brag about military prowess
and measure might in warfare.
Ask me who hates mankind?
I will point to those who
do business in ammunition
and brighten up as war darkens.
Ask me who hates mankind?
I will point to those who
preach terror and violence
and forget to spread love & peace.
Ask me who hates mankind?
I will point to those who
pull triggers and launch grenades
& decrease mankind to increase grades.
Ask me who hates mankind?
I will point to those who
prey on humans and other animals
and suck the earth pale for gains.
Ask me who hates mankind?
I will point to those who
enmesh the weak with economic strings
& suck lipids below their ancestral soils.

(Perpignan, 29 December 2016)

Man, Follow Me to Class!

Man, follow me to class
and let us learn from
the speaking silence of Nature,
and be wise. No grass ever
harms another, not even parasites, never.
But we humans strive to ruin ourselves:
we start guns that finish us;
we make bombs that mar us;
we assemble philosophies that divide us;
we resurrect sins that bury us;
we destroy nature that protects us!
Man, get your books and pens,
let's go into eco-school,
observe other beings and repent
before our world gives way. No animal ever
preys on its kind; no other animal pollutes, never.
We humans invite chaos on ourselves:
we manufacture arms that fracture us;
we adopt laws that dehumanise us;
we overstretch technology that maims us;
we ignite wars that quench us;
we evolve quickly to dissolve Nature and us!

(Perpignan, 18 September 2016)

Against Extremists

I'm against all lives in extremes.
This only puts us on one another's
throat, obscuring our reality as brothers,
bursting the sweet bubbles of our dreams.

Can't we learn from Mother Nature?
Even oceans that stretch to extremes extend
back to the land where they kiss and bend
to dance to musical notes from bands of Nature.

We need ourselves, we need one another like
dung beetles need cows to chew their food,
not as cruel cats need mice for their food.
Both cats and mice have a right to this life.

We need ourselves, we need one another to live
like plants need bees to help impregnate them,
not as wicked wolves need sheep to feed them.
Wolves and sheep all have a right to live.

Why then slash her throat for religion's sake?
It's a shame to kill life to please a lifeless ideology!
Why carry explosives to burst yourself and others
like a fowl's egg exploding in wild fires?

Why then hate them, Muslim or Christian or Buddhist,
because of their multi-named invisible Sculptor?
Brother, I invite you to peel off your religious mask
like a snake and walk forth to the aisle of humanity.
Sister, I invite you to strip off your populist mask
and rub your body against mine in a human embrace.

Syrian is just a tag, black is just a tag.
American is just a tag, white is just a tag.
Christian is just a tag, nation is just a tag.
Muslim is just a tag, refugee is just a tag.

The only real thing is you and me.
The same red blood is busy in the veins
beneath our multi-coloured skins.
The same heart drones like a car engine
behind our black or white or coloured chests.
The same air rushes in and out of our lungs.

You were born, I was born.
You will die, I will die.

This is our shared humanity.

Remove your goggles of materialism,
drop your loaded guns and reciprocate
my love held out in my open arms.
Let's intone a new human song today.

(St Andrews, 13 April 2017)

Prisons

The worst prisons
aren't four-walled dungeons
where innocent humans rot,
urinate and defecate and vomit and eat;
where light is luxury and food is finished
and torture hoisted as love flags.
The worst prisons
aren't underground oubliettes
where freedom fighters decay,
overloaded like sardine in cans,
rendered nude and sometimes raped
and beaten and washed in murky liquids.
The worst prisons
are troubled consciences
which go to war at rest time,
piercing bearers like hot thorns,
invading numbed hearts
with reminders of justice.
The worst prisons
are guilty consciences
which asphyxiate owners within,
pursuing them everywhere beneath
faces adorned with counterfeit smiles
like the pus-secreting wounds beneath
the golden suits of occultist billionaires.
The worst prisons
are restless consciences
which become screens at night,
replaying horrifying images of
innards, bones and blood from
children and adults butchered under
helpless sun and moon rays.

(St Andrews, 14 September 2017)

This Thing We Call Peace

This thing we call peace
is not only the absence of wars;
it is also when we don't trade in arms.
It is the invisible arms of a Universe
that embraces all, without discrimination.
This thing we call peace
is not only tightening security;
it is also when we need not fear again.
It is when dark shields of individuality
give way to transparent layers of collective love.
This thing we call peace
is not only ending conflicts;
it is also when brotherliness buries greed.
It is when we hold hands and smile along
the aisles of life, equalised by birth and death.
This thing we call peace
is not only the business of some;
it is also when we all grow from campaigning
for peace to practicing peace through selfless love:
loving our neighbours as ourselves, everywhere.

(St Andrews, 14 March 2017)

Six Deaths Here!

As the taxi carrying us drove past Mile 8 Akum –
between Bamenda and Santa (my destination) –
three words stroke me like the 114 deaths at Mbanga-Pongo
and the 17+ deaths on the Bafoussam-Yaoundé road.
The billboard bearing "Six Deaths Here!"
stood such that, irrespective of direction,
all careful eyes could behold it.
Its sight took me into a trance of bitter laughter.
When I came back, I wondered why all our roads
were not tarred with those words.
No place along our potholed highways
can be free of six or more deaths here or there.
Our roads are death tracks – or death triangles?
I wished that even grass in Cameroon
should be painted with those words.
The air we breathe shouldn't be left out either.
Whether we're flying, swimming, driving or walking,
safety is always far away from us in this land.
Our entire transport system is full of "X or Y Deaths Here!"
Where is our new Moses?

(Bambili, 25 May 2008)

Blood on Our Roads Every Day?

Drunk by poverty,
constipated by autocracy,
stressed by a nightmarish vie chère,
suffocated by red- and black-cap extortions,
aveuglé par vain, confusing slogans,
accursed by unburied ancestors,
constipated by commercialised permits,
disillusioned by sponsored, faithful breweries,
ensnared by serpentine hollow roads,
our chauffeurs grind countless on road mills.
Every day, innocent blood flows in barrels;
human bones crackle, break, spray marrows;
heads get crushed into shapeless meat;
eyeballs fall off sockets like blown bulbs;
stomachs tear, vomiting innards into potholes;
rampantly parked beer trucks tumble on humans;
vehicles run into others, kissing and distorting mouths;
life-sucking drivers bargain prison terms like wares
& nobody cares. King B resides in jets in foreign skies!

(Perpignan, 22 September 2016)

Family Autopsy in Public Hospital
(In loving memory of Monique Komateque & all
who die due to medical negligence in Cameroon!)

My sister respected antenatal clinic rendezvous;
she behaved as punctual as water in a waterfall.
But most of her doctors suffered from impolitetosia,
often giving her nausea and tormenting her foetuses.
On delivery day, rotten roads and money worship
pushed her into a chilly comatose.
We were tossed from one hospital to another,
for our financial frailties and insufficiencies,
under trivial pretexts of no beds, no gynaeco…
Then Monique yielded to excruciating labour pains
with her innocent twins undelivered and nobody cared.
Was I wrong when I tore her stomach for the twins?

(Mbankolo, 6 April 2016)

Healthcare Survey: Quebec versus Douala

*(In loving memory of Monique Komateque & all
who die due to medical negligence in Cameroon!)*

Healthcare in Quebec is bright
like a moonlit summer night;
with little professional flaws and ethical stains
which are causing Quebeckers less medical pains.
Healthcare in Douala is dark
like a winter night with no spark.
It is flawed by chronic negligence and love for gains
which are causing Doualas deaths and untold pains.
In Quebec healthcare payment is indirect.
Less resistance the Quebec people do erect.
Healthcare and social welfare are under one department.
Doesn't this bring the people better health development?
In Douala healthcare payment is direct.
More frustration the Douala people do eject.
Healthcare and social welfare are under different structures.
Any doubt that this causes the people many health fractures?
With RAMQ Quebec records minor weaknesses:
access concerns, doctor penury – but happiness.
Patient-doctor relations in Quebec are less and less hurtful
and service seekers in Quebec are more and more joyful.
Without RAMD Douala counts major weaknesses:
negligence, love for gains, thorny roads…breed sadness.
Patient-doctor dealings are swayed by the weight of pockets.
Many families mourn under weights of countless caskets.
Money or no money in Quebec, human life respected.
Surgeries done and care given are largely appreciated.
Family members accompany patients just as caretakers.
State plans, funds, evaluates, corrects and innovates ceaselessly.
No money in Douala, medics watch dying victims.

Labouring women, children, injured men…are all victims.
Family members butcher stomachs of dying pregnant women
in futility to save foetuses; but state ministers defend doctors?

(Mbankolo, 9 April 2016)

Wedding in Prison

"You're cordially invited
to the wedding ceremony
of Mebarato and X at Central Prison
next Saturday at 9 a.m.
Signed, Meburato, ex-embezzler."
You receive the above invitation?
Just attend, don't question because
some prisoners are more equal
than others.
Some names are like lions
and can roar in cages and forests
to the King's pleasure.
Even a dog from a royal tribe
is the king of dogs, they say.

(St Andrews, 25 March 2017)

My Brother Loved Travelling!
(In Memory of Nsah Gwain Philip,
1970 – Sunday 8 May 2016)

Soul brother! Eldest brother! Friend and brother!
You left us unannounced and in pain to travel
into eternity with no will except that I bother
about your absence to cheer me up when I travel.
In less than fifty years – just forty six years,
you sweated to carry collective burdens and travel.
You've sneaked away into glory, leaving us in tears;
but many whom you travelled to serve refused to travel!
Our moms and your wife are now widows
ever since our dad left us too in 1996 to travel.
Will there be peace in the camp of your foes?
On thorns and gravel, each of them must travel!
You mishandled our compound & your legacy seemed bleak;
almost staining dad's immortal achievements about to travel.
Fortunately, you toiled for Njinagwa projects to the peak;
sparing no effort for our health centres and schools to travel!
Your Judases and Peters flooded our compound with tears
as your dead body was laid into the last bus you took to travel.
Memories of your shoed feet pushed into the box of fears,
I shivered under weight of troubles you left to travel!

(Messa-Si, 15 July 2016)

A Fallen Colossal Building Block

(For Ma Ndim Wibua Prudentia,
2 Jan. 1949 – 16 Dec. 2016)

You were born Prudentia
and you grew into elegancia.
You were born a woman
and you reigned like a man.
You were born a daughter
and you fought like a hunter.
You were born to be a mother
and you became to many a father.
You were an umbrella for many
who will bury you in company!
Your immortal legacy for posterity
testifies how Mbesa values equality.
A colossal building block hewed out of Mbesa,
like yawning gaps Cornelius & Toah left in Mbesa!
Thank God you planted many good seeds
which will sprout and multiply your deeds!
The hands of the clock have turned round from 1986
and again punctured the Mbesa progress tyre in 2016!
You were a prayer warrior,
draped body and soul in faith
and a daring lady,
surrounded by hard-earned trophies:
daughter to teacher to mother
to SDM to Vice Principal to Principal
to MADA President to almost mayor
to Alternate Senator to Heavenly Glory...!
Your womb bore just three, but your doors were free
and you sheltered more than the leaves of a tree.
Your large and accommodating wings of a hen

wrapped many in generous warmth in times of pain.
A billionaire you never were, but invested enormously
into the studies and wellbeing of many, very selflessly.
You planted and watered prosperous seeds in and out,
despite your swarms of distractors within and without.
From Mbesa to Fiango to Bambili to Downtown,
rocks echo and re-echo the void of your departure!
For you I cannot be a troubadour or singer
because your achievements were your announcer.
Your achievements are very loud cymbals
ringing to both foes and friends as signals,
reminding us that none is an angel or perfect
since your foes want to paint you all imperfect.
You stood tall in the face of adversity
and never succumbed to traps of enmity.
Who would give me a brand new daughter
so that I name you, Mami, and
start building Downing Street in our land
to host our next Margaret Thatcher?
I may not bury you, but I can see a mammoth crowd
flooding Mbesa streets like Djue Nkong in August,
wailing, crying, sobbing, weeping to see you off, Mami;
calling you countless names as you meant a lot to countless!
Adieu, Mami! Goodbye, Ma Ndim! Safe journey, Lioness!

(Perpignan, 22 December 2016)

The Magic of Female Buttocks

African women have magnetic buttocks
which rise and fall like
erupting mountains when they dance.
Everyone is charmed by
heavy buttocks when they vibrate
to makoussa and bikutsi rhythms
like remote-controlled robots.
But who knows?
Naked eyes cannot see HIV/AIDS
when these buttocks play their magic.
Woe betides he who foolishly wets pants.
If you lose control of yourself
and develop unquenchable emotions,
you may end up in the limbo
of her Jerusalem. Beware, brother!

(Mbankolo, 27 April 2016)

Safety First

I would dodge your kiss,
be happy with my peace,
than connect fleshy lips
to become a long eclipse.
Without going for a test,
romantic life can't be best
since HIV/AIDS isn't hung
on faces but turns into dung.
I would flee naked intercourse
until we take the right course.

(St Andrews, 14 October 2017)

Glittering and Rotting

Some smooth skins we see are sour
inside, harbouring double skeletons
lodged within corporal cupboards
by those who fear or ignore anti-retro.
While they glitter outside like gold,
they rot & decompose inside like corpses.
AIDS' copious mining can be tamed
if they open up to winds of counselling.
AIDS, if not controlled, can kill for sure,
but prevention and education can cure.

(St Andrews, 14 October 2017)

I Wish I Were Born...

I

I wish I were born before 1800,
I would barricade imperialists
and spare Africa of colonial rape.
I wish I were born before 1900,
I would pierce allied hate bubbles
and spare us the 1914 genocidal avalanche.
I wish I were born before 1930,
I would abort the second grand saga
and spare Africa of imposed cobweb maps.
I wish I were born before 2000,
I wouldn't witness the legalisation of evil
and wouldn't suffocate in punitive calamities.
I wish I were born before now,
I wouldn't see people bombing selves and others
and wouldn't see freedom freed from moral prisons.

II

Suppose I was born back then,
I would be an analogue bug, unfit for android
and ostracised from the e-everything generation.
Suppose I was born back then,
I would be a horseman, unfit for air voyage
and divorced from birds that fly with people.
Suppose I was born back then,
I would use glowing faggots, not solar lamps
and stagger in darkness like serene Early Man.
Suppose I was born back then,
I would be library-bound, never consulting online
and bypass with most debates from other climes.
Suppose I was born back then,

I would forget visages soonest, no image wizardry,
and my mementoes would disappear like ghosts.

III

But since I've been born now,
je vais rater les merveilles futures:
I won't see flying houses…
But since I've been born now,
je vais rater les merveilles futures:
I won't behold rocks become cotton…
But since I've been born now,
je vais rater les merveilles futures:
I won't see man inhabit Jupiter…
But since I've been born now,
je vais rater les merveilles futures:
I won't see robots perform surgery…
But since I've been born now,
je vais rater les merveilles futures:
I won't see public nudity & coitus legalised…

(Perpignan, 20 September 2016)

A Stroll into My Past

I was born and raised by farmers
in a village on the buttocks of Mbesa hills.
From 0-7 I lived in my maternal uncle's home,
under the shades of eucalyptuses at Itinikum,
before my mother returned to our father at Njinagwa.
There we lived like sardines in tight tins:
grandma, ma and eight sons in a smoke-painted room
which served as kitchen, bedroom and storeroom.
Sometimes the ceiling was another floor!
We were very poor but spoke one language:
the language of love, unity, determination and family.
And my infant food was mainly ripe bananas.
My brothers' mouths were the grinding mills of my food:
they chewed my coco-yams with awesome dexterity.
Kola nuts picked under trees and sugarcane business
fetched the widow's mite income we survived on.
I began schooling at CBC Mbesa from 7,
already living at my dad's home at Njinagwa.
We used to march like soldiers to school to learn,
walking a distance far above four kilometres.
Sometimes we walked bare-footed on pebbled paths,
with our books and cooked food in small fibre bags.
When we closed, fresh maize stems became sugarcanes
to appease the worms rebelling for food in our tummies.
Picking fallen kola nuts and avocadoes
very early in the morning is an art we grew up with.
We would return from school straight to farms;
roasted coco-yams and sweet potatoes from moms we expected,
(somehow) in exchange for food crops and wood to carry home.
Weekends and holidays brought diverse hobbies and games:
blowing termite holes, hunting tənchuluk, making wooden bikes,

making homes within thatch-grass bundles under kola nut trees,
la'afe totosə, chufeətu-a-menkum, bing koliko, ləle tongtong,
buhnə, tang kejuin, shikə ibhəm… Wandering like a pilgrim,
I would mount Ngwa Hill, sweating under oranges, bananas
& bamboo mats to sell to the Bororos – cattle Fulani.
I would scent fresh milk as cows breastfed their young.
Stench of fresh cow dung would welcome me
while elated flies scattered over dung heaps in confusion,
bewailing frustration on my dew-wetted, dung-stained shoes.
In 96, death seized our dad from us, adding petrol to fire!
Leaving behind four wives & twenty-six children is no joke!
But for my mom, hope was all! I also cherished books,
but to some of my friends, life has been a wheel without spokes,
spewing them out like a whirlwind for reasons to me unknown.
Perched on life's wild wings I have kept sailing like a prawn,
thanking the Most High in everything I do. Or say. Or achieve.
Although my mind has mountains of troubles to displace,
it must for my childhood experiences create space.

(Perpignan, 20 September 2016)

Kola Nuts

Red, red nuts
from the high trees
in my father's compound,
I miss you and I miss life.
He who brings kola nut,
Achebe wrote, brings life.
With a bite of you
animating my mouth,
I see your parents at home,
holding their leafy hands
round my father's compound,
sheltering those birds
which are our alarm clocks.
I also see he who brings you
in fibre bags dangling under
foaming calabashes of palm wine
or nkang, escorted by buzzing bees
which produce our honey.
I also see the village soothsayer
frame your sweaters into five
pieces like your five lobes
and read the future on them –
as he throws them on the floor –
like doctors read from microscopes.

(Perpignan, 22 August 2017)

After First Rains

Be it in February or March,
first rains always brought
us joy in tons, tons of joy.
We striped ourselves naked
and ran under God's showers,
singing, dancing, shouting;
watching droplets undress
dust coats from helpless stones,
withering grass and brown roofs;
awaiting new bird songs next day.
Old activities gave way to new ones:
the search for horse-tail mesh began,
to weave into carved banana stumps
and decorate with corn-flour chaffs
to beckon births into sweet death.
Was it Ijim or Ibal-Adamu we didn't
visit uncountable times for the mesh?
Flat stones suspended above chaffs
with sticks attached to long ropes
would also ensnare birds and rat-moles
and bush fowls which loved our seeds.
Then came July and August
with fresh cobs embracing corn stems
and provoking jealousy and hunger
in countless monkeys and baboons.
It was time for scare-crowing in farms,
a time when some divorced with school
in order to save and roast potatoes and corn,
become farm masquerades for animals,
fondle with girls in hide-and-seek games
and rescue families from future famine.

(Perpignan, 25 September 2016)

39

At the Washing Machine

When my dresses unfriend cleanliness,
here in Perpignan since my arrival,
I pack them into bags or plastic papers
and to the Washing Machine I am gone.
After feeding the cash-receiving machine
with coins as demanded, I load my dresses
into the Washing Machine and move
to a nearby bench where I surrender my buttocks
and lazily watch the machine spinning like Earth
round Sun. No rest for machine, no work for me.
No physical exercise, no conversation with Nature.
Only swiftness of machine like Man's onto doom!
Except that sometimes I bury my worries
into books, books, books, and newspapers,
the best companions in individualized societies.
Back in Mbesa where I was born,
before my departure to others' lands,
when our dresses became unclean,
we would pack them into bags or basins
and carry them to rivers like Ngwa, Fenkok...
Sometimes, we trekked with children
and women – babies fastened on their backs –
balancing washing basins on their heads
and chattering, chattering, or gossiping.
We would soak our dresses in river pools,
apply soap, tap them on smooth, flat stones,
wave goodbye to dirt as it sets to travel,
squeeze and spread them on nearby grass.
For heavy blankets, two or more people
would join forces to squeeze them
in perfect communism and cheerfulness.
While elderly persons concentrated on washing,
some children played with and in water,
swimming, catching crabs and tadpoles

and selecting bullet stones for bird hunting.
It was admirable communion with Nature,
full of physical exercise, warding off diseases
and laziness as well. After chatting, planning,
washing, drying and sometimes dating,
we would baptize ourselves in cold baths
in the rivers before retiring to face the future.

(Perpignan, 23 September 2016)

Longing to Become a Baby

I wish to become a baby,
playing in water in my basins
after my baths, insulated from tragedy
by my mommy, sheltered from assassins,
swimming happily in water
gradually turning from warm to cold
like the world turning from peace to theatre,
smiling up to my busy mother, also bold.
I wish to splash water all around
as I beat water and utter meaningless words
in efforts to acquire human tongues around,
without knowing they can unite and divide: words.
And later tell mommy it is finished
each time I'm done with a ball of fufu or alang
as we gather for meals that never diminished,
unaware humanity was heading for a terror bang.

(Perpignan, 30 December 2016)

A Grandma in Big Babanki
(For my grandma and all grandmas)

By the roadside she stood,
stopping a taxi to church –
dressed in two-rope sleepers,
with a wrapper on her waist,
a headscarf on her head
and a third leg in her right hand.
Some of her grey hair laid outside
her headscarf, announcing
an age that could be numbered
with sand and dust and water.
This old mother boarded our taxi
and we helped her get in by my side.
We greeted and our taxi continued.
As I helped her hold her third leg, –
when entering and alighting –
I remembered my grandma, Veronica Teh,
who used to carry her farming nkok
on her back from Itinikum to Njinagwa,
sometimes happily barefooted yet with
shoes or two-rope sleepers in her nkok,
with her third leg too in her right hand.
She sometimes reserved ripe bananas
or avocadoes for us in her nkok
& would give us on our way to CBC Mbesa.
When for us there was no food,
she would untie one angle of her wrapper
and remove coins like 25 or 50 FCFA
to give us, especially me, for food.
Oh grandma, how I miss you!
Death cheated us and took you

when we were too young;
death snatched you from us
at an age few sticks can count!
We never saw her husband;
but she was a courageous widow
just like my mother later has been!
Same like my grandma, when this mother
alighted our taxi under about 10 minutes,
she untied a corner of her wrapper,
got 100 FCFA in coins for the driver
and branched off to PCC with other coins
to offer to God for her long life.
As she walked away to church,
again I remembered my grandma,
who was a fervent Baptist Christian –
faithful to God and our culture,
punctual, prayerful & generous to a fault.
She was a human library, a moving shelf
filled with wisdom and tales for us.
She would keep her money, nabak
and other valuables in empty milk tins.
I would collect avocadoes and give her
to keep so they get ripe and start
demanding them same day; she would
scold me, promising never to keep
my avocadoes again and would receive
me with open arms the next second!
Oh grandma, how I miss you!
Wherever you are, thanks for your love!

(Perpignan, 29 December 2016)

We Hail You, Dear Mothers!
*(For my mum and all mothers on
US Mother's Day 2017)*

We hail you, dear mothers!
God sent us through you and fathers,
who like bees fly off after dropping nectar
in you and with us inside you get fatter,
losing your freedom, with us 9 months within,
while our dads feel free without and within –
though some share with you the pain,
almost carrying their share of it for our gain.
Nine months over, worst pains you bear,
sometimes giving up your lives for ours,
or dedicating years for us alone to rear.
Good dads help you to get our food.
Like miners, we copiously drain your breasts.
But for abortionists, all mothers are so good!

(St Andrews, 14 May 2017)

Sonnet for Delphine Shang
(Dedicated to Gilbert Ndi Shang)

I respect rising stars like Delphine Shang;
brave et courageuse dame, même au champs!
Multi-tasking, this lady does with passion;
so success from God draws to her ambition.
For you, hairdressing, tailoring and school are asunder?
Then get your notebook and start looking for her!
A good sister, she remains trustworthy to her brother;
and there is no doubt she'll brighten her partner.
Quick and eager to learn!
Quick and eager to appreciate!
Quick and eager to go home
and connect with her Luh roots!
And help her mommy and daddy!
Success is flapping huge wings to her!

(Perpignan, 8 January 2017)

Abused Divine Torch

If to my home you came
to steal from me
in broad daylight
using a torch for fame –
a torch abused to cheat me,
but which shines in darkness and light!
Who is to blame: torch or thief?
Its eternal radiance illuminates souls,
though you stole it from the chosen
to soften my heart and plant mischief.
Later, you drop torch and call us fools?
A divine torch, now you want it broken!
For me, there is no turning back
from this glorious torch.
Its maker's goodness I profess.
Its maker will judge you once back
soon for abusing His divine torch.
Will you humble yourself and confess?

(St Andrews, 12 June 2017)

Sonnet for Baby Jesus

Baby Jesus in a manger
to save us from danger.
Grant more grace to me
not to join in denying thee.
Thanks for your starry birth
that bought me from death.
You weren't born exactly today,
but I am free from doomsday.
Many doubt your coming again,
but grant me that I be born again.
Strengthen my weak faith, Saviour.
Redeem any faults in my behaviour.
Many today reduce you to a fairy tale,
but your time, Oh Lamb, shall soon tell.

(Perpignan, 25 December 2016)

Two Haikus for Baby Jesus

Grant Lord that I don't
partake in auctioning you
to please the world, never.

Baby King, my heart
bleeds as many deny you
but feast like scribes.

(Perpignan, 25 December 2016)

One God, Many Ways

When at mass, priests burn incense
and I watch its smoke spiralling
like the smoke of Abel's sacrifice
into church air,
I recall traditional priests
who burn incense to warm iking
– our clay-pot gods –
when the whole family gathers.
When priests supplicate
God's angels and saints to intercede for us,
I remember aghel-ikuiking
pleading on meyiynm'abunafeyn
to send us peace and prosperity
and good sleep.
Christian priests raise bread and wine
towards heaven for communion
in remembrance of the Lamb;
Mbesa priests raise njəmtə and mehluk-məfıfınə.
From believers, priests demand confession
for sins' remission and reconciliation.
If to the altar you bring your gift
and remember a case with your sister,
drop the gift there
until you find her for reconciliation,
God's Word preaches.
When families gather round their iking,
like chicks round mother hen,
the footsteps of ngolsə-iking
dictate how they should live:
when they dance joyfully
on the saliva-triggering palm wine

in the iking clay pot
and bring their heads together,
everything is in order, there is unity;
but when they stubbornly
escape each other, sticking to pot walls,
all family members in disagreement
must continually go outside the house
and concert in reconciliation
until the snail shells nod their heads
in agreement by coming together.
Then the palm wine is served with njəmtə
like catholic communion
in celebration of family reconciliation.
For the peace Christians
share towards mass ending,
iking ceremonies end
with participants wearing fresh afu-abola
as a symbol of peace and prosperity:
it is woven into thick circles
and won like necklaces
with fresh, green leaves for beads.

(Perpignan, 18 September 2016)

PART TWO

Constimocrazy: In and Out

Forced into Oblivion

*(For 1st President of Cameroon,
Elhaj Ahmadou Ahidjo)*

Yoff Muslims' Cemetery in Dakar,
Senegal, 12th Sunday of June 2016,
in the morning, I trod across seas of dust
to pour on your tomb my buckets of tears
and clear away the labyrinth of aching fears
which have haunted me since you left in 1989
'coz we did not unfeather fowls on your tomb!
We did not tear family sackcloth after your burial.
We did not tie the gods' fowl above your corpse.
No asanghayus and burial chicken were shared
to your sons and daughters after your send-off.
You answered the call beyond our skies and seas
and were left to rot like a rat on foreign shores.
You got lost and died in a dark forest far from us?

As I walked to and fro the Graveyard,
feeding my eyes on endless blocks of adorned tombs,
my ears scanned skies in vain for your burial gunshots.
I listened attentively to the whispering silence
and heard your mid-way voice wailing for justice,
so we your kids shouldn't again be flown to see you.
We've washed our hands clean with the family calabash,
except your first son who banished you from our midst,

forcing your immortal memory into oblivion.
He exiled you like a witch without cause and fault,
but there is no one below the skies without a fault.
Have his ears turned into stones since your departure?
Perhaps, thunderous guilt has melted his eardrums!

Perhaps, the silence of your absence has deafened him!

What crime did your wife and kids commit too?
Your darling's angelic beauty is setting like the sun
on the same foreign soils where you turned into dust.
One day, even your bones' powder shall come home!

(Dakar, 12 June 2016)

King B is at it again

King B is at it again;
to modify to his gain
and leave us in silent pain.
He takes our Laws Book for a toy.
He treats us the villagers like a weak boy
since our sanity-divorced representatives make us cloy.
From our village top,
he changed from five with a stop,
without our consent, to seven without a stop.
The new figure and stop or non-stop we can't guess
given that he and his sycophants alone can curse or bless.
Without his human-dogs by our side, we can only remain helpless.
In a village where elders and nobles are blind flutists
who wine and dine with the Foyn like hired guitarists,
armless villagers must sway left-right like artists.
What shall we tell our children
as explanation for this damage, brethren,
when this desecrating Foyn becomes frozen?

(Mbankolo, 13 February 2016)

Forced to Rule

King B whirls in hospital bed.
He coughs copiously, gathers phlegm –
spits nothing – and swallows it for food.
Chandou, under forest of brown fake hair,
is attending on a golden chair at head of bed.
It is a gold-adorned Swiss private clinic.
The King casts his old eyes on a flat-screen
to check updates from his dung-beetled kingdom.
He beholds haggard thieves parading potholed roads
with motions of support forcing him to rule on.
Streams of sorrow flow down his furrowed face.
His heart splits into legions of piercing thoughts:
pity for abused masses, the war on age and sickness,
sorrow for mutilated constitutions, trillions in his coffers…
He ponders, must I be forced to rule? Forced to oppress?

(Mbankolo, 6 April 2016)

Request from King B to God

King B of CamKingdom to God:
Grant me, Oh Father, many more years
to oppress these fellows into more fears.
Let me misuse them again for some time
since their foolishness has been sublime.
God to King B of CamKingdom:
It seems you're insatiably thirsty for crimes.
Why would you table such a request at times?
King B of CamKingdom to God:
When you dictate over eternal buffoons
who applaud their rice served in tea-spoons
instead of demanding their full share in bags
and prefer to toil and wallow in smelly rags
to chant motions of support for your praises,
won't you request more time for their disgraces?
God to King B of CamKingdom:
It seems you take glory in their stupidities.
Why would you keep exploiting their naiveties?
King B of CamKingdom to God:
When you misappropriate a people's funds
and deceive them to imprison others for funds,
you'd have no choice but to treat them like dogs
so that they wag tails to your family as real dogs.
They misdirect all what they have which is God's
and treat me and my family as benevolent gods.
God to King B of CamKingdom:
It seems you've a voracious appetite for power.
Why would you overstretch my forgiving power?
King B of CamKingdom to God:
Lord, with some of them awful things I've done
and they shall not be forgiven when I am gone.

Reason why they want their constitution amended
to cover them till all of us shall have transcended
to plead for mercies at the footstool of your Throne
and leave our children to shed blood over the throne.
God to King B of CamKingdom:
It seems you've a soaring thirst for corruption.
Why would you want to beg for my compassion?
King B of CamKingdom to God:
Lord, why won't I make use of this advantage
when they sing my glories despite my old age?
They have christened me their natural candidate.
For salvation, won't I also be a natural candidate?

(Mbankolo, 16 April 2016)

Roads Blocked for the King

After hectic working days –
or very early before we go to work –
countless human dogs mount barricades
to people: students, workers, patients, diplomats –
for sit-glued King to make endless trips across shores.
Our economy withers like a dry-season plant in the Sahel.
Yesterday roads were blocked again!
In a cab we wound through Tosbas to main road.
A human dog draped in khakis like a religious rebel
skipped into road like a cat – bullets on waist, gun at hand.
Like a trained chorister, he conducted us to a sudden stop,
ready to blow us if our driver dare to cross where he stood.
After waiting for too long,
our driver turned around to try elsewhere
at Round Point – again to no avail, no way to pass.
We advised hungry pupils in the cab to trek home and eat.
Lady on my left kept sighing and cursing, cursing and sighing:
regime of slogans, godification, inertia and theft.
Old man near the driver fell asleep.
He woke up and nothing had changed: we stood still!
He removed his cap, quickly scratched his mooned head
and cursed: "Nous sommes encore ici? Maudit!"
Explosion of laughter; private car driver nearby laughed highest.
Old man alighted to trek home, cursing and cursing.
Out through taxi window,
we sighted a man returning from work –
exhausted, with his coat held in hand, trekking uphill.
He cursed and smiled, smiled and cursed as he trekked.
Endlessly we laughed, all of us victims.
He consoled: "On est déjà habitué! Pas de choix!"

(Mbankolo, 20 April 2016)

Mandate Emergency

Hung-hong! Hung-hong! Hung-hong!
Sirens! Sirens! Sirens! Sirens! Sirens!
Emergency at United Palace Theatre:
King B quakes in bed, almost dying.
Mandate soon elapsing, emergency!
Former-crown-monger-turned-town-crier
summons legal medics in sashes
who applaud as the King's virus
is hauled in on a stretcher
to be operated upon.
Adorned in Kingdom tricolours
and wheeled across the hall
amidst loud ovations
is our Constitution
whose last limbs
will be mutilated to ensure
King B reigns forever
while others bleed!

(St Andrews, 15 May 2017)

Executive Mandates

In any country on earth,
once political surgeons
butcher limits to executive mandates,
using the term constitution becomes
a democratic blasphemy,
a constitutional sacrilege,
a political abomination,
a demoncrazic neologism,
a dictatorial normalcy.
No limits on mandates means
as long as I am alive
and can rig.
Now I am king; wait until I go.
Worst is when electoral organ
is subsection of a royal party;
when all village titleholders
pay blind allegiance to Igwe
and are obliged to meddle in
feather counting. Can add feathers!
Aren't they landlords? Civil chefs!
And we keep renting our land!
In such contexts,
ballots lose their validity;
they become as useless as
raised fingers of a corpse
in a family meeting.
Going to polls loses its allure;
it becomes sheer rehearsal
until when democracy rises again
like Jesus Christ
or when Igwe gets missing.
Long live the King!

(St Andrews, 2 July 2017)

Imported Feathers

The King's mandate
is said to rotate in our village,
but it never really does.
Our King is so wise
or our kingmakers are foolish,
I guess. Or they say.
When a mandate expires,
we use feathers to choose
our next King, who is same since.
When this time comes,
King B orders cartons of fake feathers
from villages across big streams
and warns all Manjong leaders
on all entry points to our village
to stay quiet, lest they lose their jobs
or have no goodbyes for their families.
There is just no way to change this king!
Not even with kingmakers and elders?
The ones whose fibre bags are swelled
with royal champagnes before campaigns?
A general march to gather under the fig tree
in the middle of our village may help,
if anti-gathering dogs regain their sanity!

(St Andrews, 15 May 2017)

The Difference

As you see us free and fresh,
it is not that we didn't soil our hands.
We also burst village calabashes underneath
and connected some collective palm wine
into our family gourds
at home and abroad.
But when we bend down to burst,
we close our eyes from the royal tusks
so we can clasp oil-stained hands
to worship His Highness.
As you see us tied and whipped on pillars
Inside Kfifoyn's compound, it is not only that
we dipped our invisible fingers into village oils.
We and all other nchindas scurried village kola-nuts
into our fibre bags
in the village and beyond.
But when we bent down to swindle,
our eyes lingered to admire our royal cowries
and our hearts wondered when His Highness
will take his rest for others to reign.

(Perpignan, 12 November 2016)

From Chief to Thief

Our chief flew abroad without rests
and littered our village with nests
instead of durable mansions like
those he lived in abroad; wife alike.
Of nothing was he really abreast
except pointing patriots for arrest.
Our village was rotting from inside
like a fallen pawpaw; chief aside.
Brothers across the river, on request,
swallowed us like amoeba in quest
of food; and we triggered unrest
throughout the village to have a rest.
Instead of beating the rallying gong
under the friendship tree, a bong
of sorrow on us he began to land.
Then red rivers flooded our land
till other villages saw our weird situation
and came to help us in consolation!
They spared us the pangs of the thief
and joined us enthrone our own chief.

(St Andrews, 24 January 2017)

Roads of Emergence

Abreast yourself for turbulence.
Adorn yourself in iron boots and steel attire.
Let's ride on our roads of emergence.
No ease and fun till we retire.
Yaoundé-Bafoussam
Width of a bed: zigzag, zigzag, zigzag
Holes, holes, holes the size of mass coffins
Checkpoints, checkpoints, checkpoints like sand
Tar in parches, tar in parches, tar in parches
Bafoussam-Bamenda
Breath of a pen: zigzag, zigzag, zigzag
Holes, holes, holes the size of mass graves
Red and black caps; whistles, five hundred
Truncated paths; tar here, mud there, dust here
Yaoundé-Douala
Width of a thread: zigzag, zigzag, zigzag
Holes, holes, holes the size of mass hearses
Drunk drivers, old timber trucks, money whistles
Tar and earth, tar and earth, tar and earth
Belo-Mbesa
Thin footpath: zigzag, zigzag, zigzag
Holes, stones, rocks, mud, gutters the size of mass mortuaries
Exhausted motorcycles, wailing land-rovers, money whistles
No tar, no cement; only earth, only earth: mud and dust
Emana-Monatélé
Breadth of a hair: zigzag, zigzag, zigzag
Potholes, potholes, potholes the size of mass cemeteries
Dancing into empty holes, galloping into road-lakes
Tar and earth, gravel and sand, checkpoints, money whistles

Plied by republican zombies and parasites
to write motions of support for our submergence
How do we transport patients and pregnant women?
The old King they force to stay may answer.

(Mbankolo, 9 April 2016)

My Origins

I was born in fertile forests
where we toyed with reindeers,
but our leaders have smeared the forests
with sterility and intoxicated us with beers.
I was born in productive plains
where webcams are dreaded like terrorists,
but our leaders take delight in buying planes
and take those levelling fields for anarchists.
I was born in an aping community
where statistics are cooked like cow meat
since our leaders hide skeletons from society
and peel off enemies' skins when they meet.
I was born in rubber and banana plantations
where my people toil and wave oil-loaded lorries
driving across River Mango to fuel vain ambitions,
and swell pockets for our immortal King's glories.

(Perpignan, 12 November 2016)

To Ex-Grandma on Her Divorce

Dear Ex-Grandma,
Our spring of sentiments got dried after your divorce,
your breakaway from your sister-wives without force
recently. Freedom is good, but no excess. You see?
You swooped down on us as a mom beyond the sea
many years ago, and tortured us with an iron hand,
desecrating and confiscating our ancestral land.
You auctioned us to our sisters in a bubbling union
of servitude – sweating for sisters – without our opinion.
We're now orphans, washing our sisters' dirty dishes
and gun-pointed each time we say they take us for fishes.
Our sisters have turned us into their kids, you know?
The union you loathe now wasn't forced on you, we know.
But you deceived us into an incestuous, barren relation.
And on your divorce you expect us to say congratulations?
No. No way! Except you promise to unclaw us from ours.
No. No way! Except we're freed from this prison within hours.
By the way, you've left a large, free compound to be alone,
but we need our freedom to cooperate, not to stand alone.
Many neighbours fear you'll soon catch colds and crumble,
but all we want is our own freedom. Don't make us grumble!
Thanks in advance for contacting your sister-sellers to free us;
Otherwise, ...!
Coldest regards,
Your Forced Ex-Children.

(Perpignan, 30 September 2016)

To Those Sent Against Their Own Blood

Listen to me, soul brother!
Point not your AK-47 at me,
the enemy has sent you.
We are not enemies, brother.
They sip foreign champagne,
flash silver teeth from abroad,
mock you with coins for wages,
urge you to spill your own blood,
and laugh your ignorance behind.
You'll gain nothing if we fall.
Listen to me, soul sister!
Drop not your tear gas on me,
our enemy manipulates you.
We are not enemies, sister.
They've plundered our wealth,
wiped anuses with our complaints,
filled foreign barns with our maize
and sent you in tattered boots to kill.
You'll gain nothing if we fall.
Can I talk to you, soul brethren?
Did you see the potholed paths you
drove on to butcher us, your people?
The budget has swelled their pockets
like those of a nursing kangaroo.
For half a century, they've won wax
on their eyes and ears, pushing us here.
If they stoop, good; if we part ways, better.
But be assured, our kids' future will be best.
Beware of innocent blood and ancestral wrath!

(Perpignan, 21 November 2016)

To Unknown Kinsmen

My dearest kinsmen,
I salute your bravery and integrity.
Welcome out of their forest,
but the river is still ahead.
In the air, gushing sounds of flood,
but our hands shouldn't touch blood.
Our family compound
is still as you left, no big change,
except some pretentious clearings.
Do you know they finally saw their faults
but pride hasn't allowed them to bow?
Our compound still needs cleansing,
especially as some family oracles
were fed to fishes in your absence.
Whether we gather round our ancestral pot
or fall apart like Achebe's book,
we still need cleansing and rinsing.
We still have battles to win,
and our measurements of victory
must be the happiness of all
when we gather as equal children
and smear our faces with stew
from family plates in equal portions,
no child eating more than others.
No child dishing out orders to others.
(Not that we throw age to dogs!)
Only us living as polygamous brothers.

(Perpignan, 30 August 2017)

Football and Referees

Although I am not
a good fan of football,
I admire bad referees;
they're so good.
They keep committing errors,
taking half measures
and prolonging matches
until real winners win
or real losers lose
the match. Let all matches
be handled by bad referees
so winners smile,
so winners celebrate,
so winners kiss trophies.

(Perpignan, 1 September 2017)

Jigger Epidemic

The jiggers of resistance
lodged in our left foot
when our two feet were forced
into one fake foot
with hypocritical ropes of oneness.
As one body on two feet,
we walked and worked well.
But since the seventy-two jigger epidemic,
we limp like lame lions.
Yes, we limp like ngoin-mbuhseh!
Whenever right foot pretends to ignore
sweet pains from the jiggers bulldozing within,
the determined diggers dish
out urine to announce their presence.
The latest urine silently glides down
our flesh like hot tears
on Mount Fako, instilling fears,
ready to restore our two feet
or to break body bridges.

(St Andrews, 17 September 2017)

Dogs
(Translated from Mbesa version)

We are dogs –
as you said, as you called –
because you're snatching our bone.
If you hate dogs,
flee from bones.
You kill people like animals in a forest,
crackle bones like wolves,
lick marrow like mad dogs,
drink blood like mosquitoes in Tiko,
and call us dogs?
King of dogs,
you can't snatch a fowl's grasshopper
because you deem the fowl small,
let me remind you,
leader of thieving dogs.

(St Andrews, 29 September 2017)

Where Do We Hide?

Since when did our identity
become a crime?
Perhaps because our identity
is composed like compost?
It is the dotted skin of a giraffe:
Anglo and Afro dots,
white and black spots.
For crying loud
that our brothers across the rive
are engulfing our being like amoebae,
we've been hemmed in on all sides:
tear gas,
water cannons,
Kalashnikovs,
AK47s…
Then burst skulls, marrow on roads.
Then broken limbs, blood taps gush.
Then students' pelvises open, rape, rape.
Then innocent kids at home, stray bullets.
Havoc, havoc, havoc, havoc…
Today we're dialogue partners,
tomorrow we're branded terrorists
as you bring ropes to name
the dog chosen for hanging.
We're innocent dogs, beware our blood!
You've turned off lights,
stopped us from clickology
and postology
so the world doesn't
see you strangle us.
On you, our vomit, shit

and blood will be the mark of Cain.
Beware, the man splitting wood in the moon!
Beware, God watches!
We'll escape
and be free.

(St Andrews, 24 January 2017)

We Long For Longer Days

(Celebrating World Book Day 2017)

We wish you return later, Evening,
so we live in one long beginning.
For some time now, when night falls,
masked brothers kick us like balls
and gun-point us to dark, hungry cars
bound for far forests to inscribe scars
on us and add us to others in that grave
in which maggots feast on our brave.
We long for longer days and no nights.
Often, we hear Mount Fako wailing
as our people's voices fade out across
ghostly valleys suffering venomous bites
from human-headed gaunt dogs executing
heinous orders on those carrying our cross.

(St Andrews, 2 March 2017)

Orphans with Parents

We're orphans with parents:
we're denied residence at home
by a father who call us bastards
for singing songs of our brotherhood
and reminding our brothers we're equal.
Our dad is unfit for polygamy,
but enticed our mom into marriage
many, many years ago.
He forced our step-mom's name on us,
sent her children to confuse our tongue,
refused us from speaking our mom's tongue
and visiting our kindred in her village.
But those kids brag about their mom's culture,
snatch our palm oil for their own kindred.
Worst still, dad said we should close mom's house
and come over to their mom's house.
We're now tenants in our compound.
Is their mom his wife or their husband?
And when we wail to neighbours' compounds,
he comes telling them we want to sell his plot.
That we want to divide his family,
as if polygamists can divorce division.
Why didn't he go for one wife then?
Two can never be one;
they can only form two-in-one
if cultivated on love and equality manure.
Otherwise, weeds of tensions and divisions sprout.

(St Andrews, 25 March 2017)

We Know It Very Well!

You can chop it
on a kitchen chopping board
and share it to you children
for their dinner.
We know it very well!
Even our neighbours know it!
We know it very well;
like a giant-rat knows its hole:
whether at dawn or at dusk,
it never misses it.

You can slice it
like meat on a slicing board
and divide it among your guests
for their supper.
We know it very well!
Even our neighbours know it!
We know it very well;
like a bee knows its hive:
whether from far or near nectar hunts,
it never misses it.

You can cut it
like egusi pudding in a plate
and share to your wives and concubines
for their birthday cake.
We know it very well!
Even our neighbours know it!
We know it very well;
like a person knows their mouth:
whether eating in light or darkness,

they never miss it.

We know each and every inch of it.
We know where it begins and ends.
We know where and how we got it:
an inheritance from our parents,
before you lured them to your abattoir
of brotherliness. Of love and unity?

Yes! Yes, we're beasts of no nation,
but not beasts of no land.
We're an insoluble grain of sand,
the stubborn grain of Obasijom nation.

You can swallow it
in your bottomless stomach
like a viper for your breakfast.
You'll either vomit it like a bat
or defecate it as solid as the sand
in the gizzard of a village fowl.

You can grind it
on your grinding stone
into fine powder for fertilizing your farms.
You'll either separate it for aeon years
from your crops or sweep it away
for it will be stubborn sand in your tapioca.

You can bottle it
in non-degradable plastic bottles
like mineral water and transport it to far lands.
You'll either hire chemists to separate it
or face the blessings of its intoxication
for it will be as immiscible as water & kerosene.

We know each and every inch of it.
We know its depth and breadth.
We know to whom to bequeath it:
an inheritance to our children,
free from the bloody stains of oppression
after our torture has lighted their path to freedom.

Yes! Yes, we're beasts of no nation,
but not beasts of no land.
We're an insoluble grain of sand,
the stubborn grain of Obasijom nation.

(St Andrews, 26 January 2017)

People for Sale

Here,
buy one, take two.
Buy two, take four.
For here yi cheap. People
for sale, by their own folk.
People on auction like rotting mangoes,
auctioned by their own blood
for greed.
Buy four, take sixteen.
By twenty, take two million.
For here yi cheap. Better na rain.
Market no di pass; I can't miss next reshuffle.
People washed in cold blood
like slaughtered cows in an abattoir
for auction in markets of interests!
Brisk business with
slave buyers
from across
the Mango Stream.

(St Andrews, 12 February 2017)

Welcome to Peaceland!

Welcome to a peace haven
where bullets on brother bodies
are signposts of no war.
Feel free in our fat-fees
campuses
where
butts
reinforce lessons.
'No violence! No violence!'
Students chant in Buea,
but human bees from Yaoundé
invade them, stinging with bullets,
rubbing students in dark-greyish
polls of stagnant water,
ransacking hostels,
tearing female panties
to deposit bitter honey,
while vice chancellor
whirls on golden seat
celebrating victory
and eyeing next
shakeup.

(St Andrews, 12 February 2017)

Of Law

We all must not read law
to interpret it. What's law?
Law must be for majority,
for collective; but not for individual.
Law that broke an earlier law
is no law.
Law implemented in segments
is no law.
Law spinning on an axis for pleasure
of an individual and displeasure
of a majority is nonsense.
It isn't law; it's low!
Law that drags human dignity in mud
is the famous gold ring on a pig's nose.
The best law is love;
the best lawyer is truth
and the best judge is God.
You want the worst law?
Ask a despot.

(St Andrews, 24 January 2017)

Can a Jurist Help?

How lawful
is a law
that broke an existing law
before becoming law
to keep the weak low?
How painful
are the pains
inflicted on people in pains
who decry the laws that create pains
on the weak with no fear for pens?
How awful
is it to apply bad laws in bits
by the one who eats all fleshy bits
of meat from the weak he beats?

(St Andrews, 22 February 2017)

For Freedom Fair

If those dining and wining with oppressors
convene a global exhibition of freedoms,
we'll bring along these awesome portraits:
Ibrahim with legs sharpened like a pencil,
his hanging dried bones an indelible lead.
Boys and girls baptized in pools of mud
and rubbed with slaps in rapacious beds
by rogues hiding libidinal greed in uniforms.
Battered jurists watching their wigs seized
by hawks who know Canon more than Popes.
Lifeless bodies of youth stretchered on ladders,
shattered skulls watering roads for emergence.
Pregnant women ignored on verandas for money
or with stomachs sliced by relatives for foetuses.

(St Andrews, 25 March 2017)

African Resources

If African gold and other minerals
were hanging down on trees like fruits,
foreign swarms of locusts would've
striped them naked of fruits and leaves,
leaving the trees withered like Jesus' fig.
If African trees weren't ground-anchored
but floated in air like rainy-season clouds,
foreign automated harvesters would've flown in,
chewing them here and vomiting them abroad,
leaving us emaciated like kwashiorkor patients.
If African oil wells weren't lodged underground
but fell from above like July raindrops,
foreign metallic mouths would've come
sucking them here and urinating them elsewhere,
leaving their owners pale like AIDS victims.
Luckily, God wedged these riches
beneath or on African ground;
and we often see them carried away,
as we fight and starve to death behind.
Sometimes, we don't even see
as they're stolen under cover of night,
simultaneously accompanying their prices
to distant tax havens for our thieving-chiefs.

(St Andrews, 11 June 2017)

Boundaries in Africa

We are not against boundaries
since Nature has them everywhere:
rivers, seas, cliffs, valleys, mountains.
But boundaries pencilled on scrolls
in Berlin do not help us, do not help us.
They divide us, they ruin us, they kill us.
They're cobwebs knitted by foreign spiders
that came like locusts for our gold and timber.
They're labyrinths of impenetrable spirals
splattered across our land by wealth beetles.
They're trails of duck feet stamped on mud;
stamped by wise ducks scampering for worms.
They're imaginary lines, sharper than razorblades,
that split brothers apart, filed by strange tongues.

(St Andrews, 24 March 2017)

African Democracies

If you tear or burn a piece of cloth: treason.
Swindle sums, mutilate constitutions: reason.
In Africa, power dodges ballot boxes;
but is transferred from fathers to sons.
They own nations like private boxes
and throw all who raise brows in prisons.
Some offered power on golden platters free of charge
glue themselves to thrones and swear never to discharge.
Rulers concede defeats, congratulate winners,
and later change their minds like daydreamers.
Articles demanding asset declarations
suffer intolerable, disgusting humiliations;
but mandate-limit modifications
send hand clappers into thunderous acclamations.
I pity mandate-limiting articles in our constitutions:
opened and stitched like in caesarean operations!
When mandates elapse, power lovers
postpone elections and claw protesters.
Federations swallowed for personal gratification,
but secession is taboo for an entire population.
Rulers from foreign hotels come to rule in planes
instead of ploughing and investing on our plains.
When western leaders visit us they spend days,
but most of our rulers go there for holidays.
Soldier ants surround them with gunned fences
against unarmed populations accused of offenses.
Roads blocked each time they go visiting
to save what they have been stealing.
Sick rulers flown to foreign hospitals
as citizens suffocate in rotting local hospitals.

(Perpignan, 23 December 2016)

Constimocrazy

Some spoons of communalism –
people for people, people thinking people –
could adorn but not stain it here.
Some pinches of our ancestral values –
heeding morality gongs, listening to Nature –
could spice but not spoil it here.
But we've overdosed it with wild,
weird condiments; turning it into corn-chaff
in trembling hands of professional amateurs.
It now constipates like rotting meat and bitter-leaves.
Its codes continuously modified to suit Chief Cook
and displease the people it is stewed for,
leaving them hungry like Christians who visited Satan
and could not stand the smell of cooked human blood.
It's constitutional modification democracy!
It's a birthday cake for throne-glued old kings,
made of shit, shame, garbage, greed and okra,
wrapped in opaque napkins of demoncrazy,
above which is inscribed CONSTIPÉ,
signed by an artiste who found death abroad.

(St Andrews, 12 March 2017)

Constimocrazic Thermometers

How do we read constimocrazic thermometers?
In any constimocrazy,
there is a drought of democracy:
electoral fraud, personality cults, endemic amendments,
limitless mandates, repression of opposition, imprisonments.
Executions and torture top dictatorship speedometers.

How do we measure constimocrazic temperatures?
In any constimocrazy,
there is no room for democracy:
military budgets sink into anti-protest tankers
while sycophants and their bosses become bankers
and reduce helpless civilians to wretched creatures.

How do we identify constimocrazic governments?
In any constimocrazy,
we sense odours of gerontocracy:
leadership roles are sold to grave-awaiting fellows
who embezzle and turn youths into clandestine sailors.
Like Iscariot, they betray masses in awkward arrangements.

How do we pinpoint constimocrazic zones?
In any constimocrazy,
we see the fangs of autocracy:
constitutions are changed like kids change toys.
Every adversary is charged and arrested for ploys.
Black clouds of oppression move in all horizons.

How do we demarcate constimocrazic systems?
In any constimocrazy,
there are scents of aristocracy:

speeches are made in tyrant's name as prayers,
from start to end by brainwashed and scared betrayers.
Inertia & incompetence parade in such angelic systems.

How do we recognise constimocrazic regimes?
In any constimocracy,
there is rampant artificial illiteracy:
half brains are manipulated through vain slogans.
Progress is paper-bound in all stagnant public organs.
Falsehood, champagne parties…mark out such regimes.

(Mbankolo, 10 April 2016)

Sonnet for Dictators

After polls, all governments are a dictating minority,
but chosen by and answerable to electoral majority.
Transparently chosen ones can't skip the fence of law,
except those who mutilate and bring constitutions low,
reducing collective laws into disposable toilet tissue
where mandate-limiting clauses are no longer an issue.
In our black continent, all dictators are saintly devils,
but some are better; development conceals their evils.

Such are desirable; let's call them fertile dictators.
They're so rare! Rare like gold! You need examples?
Don't ask why we're still in black, mourning Gaddafi.
Economically barren dictators are worst; bloody parasites!
They flood our continent. Slogan machines. Want some?
Hmm! Hmm! No me oh! Better ask the Monetary Fund!

(St Andrews, 1 July 2017)

Security

(For Bishop Balla)

Security
is when armed battalions
guard a corpse strangled in
insecurity.

Security
is when wolves wag tails to graves
but can't trace the slaughterhouse of
obscurity.

Security
is when we waste in hiring surgeons
to bandage wounds from a hidden
atrocity.

(Perpignan, 2 August 2017)

Interests

Interests control all our actions and feelings.
Interests are the irresistible currents of desire
which forever sweep along all human dealings.
On egoistic soils, they spread like dry-season fire.
Their manure is greedy like coconut peelings.
Interests are the creatures behind all masks:
aid masks, love masks, peace masks, work masks.
Interests underpin both friendships and conflicts:
interests start, promote, sustain and end conflicts.
You remember Libya? You remember Syria?
Great leaders pursue great, great gains and interests.
Common people have their own gains and interests.
Everywhere, interests, interests, interests – but hidden.
Interests had Gaddafi and Libyans killed and beaten.
Interests glue and scatter Obamas, Camerons, Puttins.
Business gurus chase interests, banks follow interests.
Politicians hunt interests, philanthropists have interests.
Material interests, spiritual interests, everywhere interests.
People sold and bought, healed and killed for interests.
Africa is a victim of interests, with her own interests.
Sometimes interests are calm like dormant volcanoes.
Sometimes interests show their ugly head like woes.
Givers give with interests, takers take with interests.
The Unseen Being moulded the world with interests.
Interests inspire the deeds of both cowards and heroes.
No interests no wars? No wars no interests? Interests.
No interests no allies? No allies no interests? Interests.
No interest no killings? No killings no interests? Interests.
No interests no action? No action no interests? Interests.
No interests no world? No world no interests? Interests.

(Mbankolo, 11 April 2016)

On the Middle of a Hammock

The land of the Great Dream
now hangs on middle of a hammock,
dangling across an unseen stream,
heralding hope and possible havoc
for some and for others – but time
alone will tell which direction new pilot
takes. Greatness for him is now prime!
For any mess made, beware the ballot!
Clouds of doubt spreading above US skies?
No need for doubt, Trump trusts our God.
He can never crush you like common flies.
Don't you profess trust in a certain God?
He crawls under wings of a Stable Constitution
which is bitter for any violation or modification.

(St Andrews, 25 January 2017)

Miles and Missiles

Happy on slippery war hill,
preparing to maim and kill,
caressing and kissing bombs
which will transport us to tombs.
No reason in his heart and head
as he targets Guam Island ahead,
measuring miles, miles, miles
to shave with merciless missiles.

Comfortably lodged behind oval table,
blind to this world becoming unstable,
he sends waves of fire and fury afar.
Rubble and corpses are no more far.
Weapon makers beam with smiles,
awaiting cash which flows in missiles.
We the poor will waste more blood
while soldiers surround them like a flood.

(Perpignan, 13 August 2017)

THE END

ACKNOWLEDGMENTS

Some of the poems in this collection first appeared in an-
thologies and magazines around the globe. As far as I can
remember, I would like to acknowledge them (being aware
that some may be forthcoming). The quote that opens the
collection and the poem 'The Torch Ahead' first appeared
in an Indian anthology entitled *Hope Reborn* in 2016. The
following poems first appeared in magazines: 'Healthcare
Survey: Douala versus Quebec' in *Stories for Humanity*;
'Executive Mandates' in *Spillwords Press*; 'My Origins,'
'I Jogged into Mother Nature' and 'Against Extremists' in
Scarlet Leaf Review; 'Welcome to Peaceland!' in *Dissident
Voice;* 'African Resources* (as 'The Location of African
Resources') and 'To Those Sent Against Their Own Blood'
in *Tuck Magazine.*

Pski's Porch Publishing was formed July 2012, to make books for people who like people who like books. We hope we have some small successes. **www.pskisporch.com**.

323 East Avenue
Lockport, NY 14094
www.pskisporch.com

Made in the USA
Middletown, DE
22 January 2018